painting
without
brushes

Painting with leaves, hands, wellies and more

ges
-5

Author
Brenda Whittle

Editor
Victoria Lee

Assistant Editor
Rachel Mackinnon

Series Designer
Anna Oliwa

Designer
Yen Fu and
Anna Oliwa

Cover Illustration
Craig Cameron/
The Art Collection

Illustrations
Debbie Clark

Text © 2007 Brenda Whittle
© 2007 Scholastic Ltd

Designed using Adobe InDesign

Published by Scholastic Ltd
Villiers House
Clarendon Avenue
Leamington Spa
Warwickshire
CV32 5PR
www.scholastic.co.uk

Printed by Bell and Bain

1 2 3 4 5 6 7 8 9   7 8 9 0 1 2 3 4 5 6

British Library Cataloguing-in-Publication Data
A catalogue record for this book is available from the British Library.

ISBN 0-439-94515-1
ISBN 978-0439-94515-8

With thanks to Heidi Jayne for her creative ideas, expertise and support in the production of this book.

Acknowledgements

The publishers gratefully acknowledge permission to reproduce the following copyright material:
Marie Brookes for the use of 'My Goldfish' by Marie Brookes from *Yellow Poetry Paintbox* chosen by John Foster © 1994, Marie Brookes (1994, Oxford University Press).

Qualifications and Curriculum Authority for the uses of extracts from the QCA/DfEE document Curriculum Guidance for the Foundation Stage © 2000 Qualifications and Curriculum Authority.
Every effort has been made to trace copyright holders for the works reproduced in this book, and the publishers apologise for any inadvertent omissions.

Due to the nature of the web, we cannot guarantee the content or links of any site mentioned. We strongly recommend that teachers check websites before using them in the classroom.

Contents

Exploring paint

Reasons for painting

Pushing the boundaries

Introduction

Painting without brushes

Painting without brushes is one of a series of books containing 'outside the box' ideas for practitioners working with children in the early years. The activities in this series are written with children's interests and joy for life at their very heart, bearing in mind that children love to be doing, investigating, making, creating and solving problems. They are designed to excite and stimulate children as they learn through using their senses, being active and thinking for themselves.

But why painting without brushes?

Dispensing with brushes makes you think. It makes you look again at what you are doing and the painting opportunities you are offering. Children are naturally creative, they love variety and respond to exciting new experiences, but their creativity needs nurturing and treating with respect. Children can easily be turned off drawing and painting from a very early age, saying that they are 'no good at art'. The aim of this book is to provide ideas for joyful painting opportunities to inspire children of all abilities. The activities are designed to give

practitioners ideas to offer a wide variety of painting experiences in creative, imaginative and role play situations indoors and outside. They are not discrete painting activities, but integrated cross-curricular activities with painting as their focus.

Wanting to paint

The activities are designed to stimulate children's imaginations, to encourage them to think, experiment and reflect, but most of all to inspire them to want to paint. In order to widen children's experiences and keep their enthusiasm for painting alive, a wide variety of paints are used in the activities, from colour washes to powder paints thickened with sand and glue or sparkling with glitter.

How to use this book

The book is organised in three sections:
● Chapter 1: 'Exploring paint' includes activities to introduce very young children, who may never have touched paint before, to varied activities where they delight in using their senses as they mix colours with their fingers, roll tubes and balls in paint, or discover the properties of coloured foam as

they use it to paint walls and fences. They paint coloured washes using herbs, and paint flowers by dipping their hands in scented paints.

● Chapter 2: 'Reasons for painting' covers theme-based activities designed to draw children in and fire their imaginations. They may participate through role play as bricklayers wearing hard hats, making magic paints using magic recipes and wands, or as house painters covering cracks in a wall with thick paint. They dance to music and paint what they hear and feel, or make and paint their own racetrack for toy cars.

● Chapter 3: 'Pushing the boundaries' includes painting activities that do not involve paint. These are designed to give practitioners ideas of different ways of looking at 'painting' a picture, and to encourage both practitioners and children to open their minds and be free to be creative and innovative. The ideas are very varied, ranging from making designs in melted chocolate, to painting with lengths of fabric or being part of a living painting.

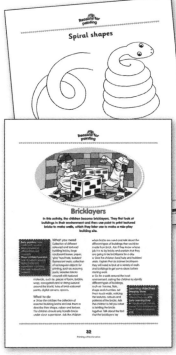

The activities
Planning and learning objectives
Links to the Stepping Stones and Early Learning Goals for Creative development in the QCA document *Curriculum guidance for the foundation stage* are shown for each activity to aid planning. The activities are all cross-curricular and the main link to one of the other five Areas of Learning is also shown.

Support and extension
Each activity has suggestions for practitioners to adapt or extend the activities according to children's needs and stage of development.

Assessment
Practitioners can assess children against the Stepping Stones and Early Learning Goals shown for each activity. Most of the activities are designed for small groups, enabling practitioners to observe individual children's progress and aid assessment to inform future planning.

Further activities
These provide more suggestions for developing lively activities linked to the main activity.

Play links
Ideas for play linked to the main activity are given to continue the theme into other Areas of Learning, such as opportunities for investigations or role play.

Home links
In order to promote and foster a partnership with parents or carers for the benefit of the children, a suggestion is given in each activity to link the learning in the setting to that in the home.

Health and safety
When working outside, always check that the area is clean and safe and that children wash their hands after collecting items such as leaves. Check that children do not have any allergies before they taste foods or touch plants or substances such as glues, shaving foam, perfumes or paints.

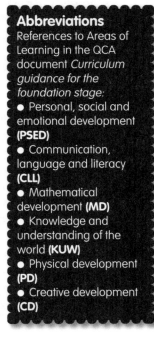

Abbreviations
References to Areas of Learning in the QCA document *Curriculum guidance for the foundation stage:*
● Personal, social and emotional development **(PSED)**
● Communication, language and literacy **(CLL)**
● Mathematical development **(MD)**
● Knowledge and understanding of the world **(KUW)**
● Physical development **(PD)**
● Creative development **(CD)**

Exploring paint

Early painting

The children experiment freely with finger-paint on a table top, discovering its qualities and mixing colours, making patterns and even taking prints of their work.

What you need
Table top; finger-paints; paper; hand-washing facilities; aprons.

What to do
● Put generous amounts of finger-paints, in different colours, on a table. Before starting the activity ensure the children put aprons on. Ask them to spread the finger-paints over the table top with their hands, enjoying the 'feel' of the paint. Ask them to tell you which colours they are using.
● Encourage the children to describe what they see and what the paint feels like. If their hands are covered in different coloured paint and they rub them together, what happens?
● Ask the children to see if they can make patterns in the paint using their fingers. They could:
  ● draw using one finger
  ● make marks with their knuckles
  ● make thumb or fingerprints
  ● drag their fingers through the paint like a comb.
● At any stage, the children can take a print of their work by laying a piece of paper over it and pressing down, or they can just enjoy the painting experience.

Early painters have the opportunity to experience the tactile qualities of paint and the joys of colour and pattern. **More confident painters** experiment in making patterns with their hands and in mixing colours.

Learning objectives
Stepping Stones
● Begin to differentiate colours. **(CD)**
● Differentiate marks and movements on paper. **(CD)**
● Explore what happens when they mix colours. **(CD)**
Early Learning Goal
● Explore colour, texture, shape, form and space in two or three dimensions. **(CD)**

Support and extension
● Younger children may be reluctant to get 'messy' and may not like the feeling of the paint on their hands. Be sensitive to their feelings and encourage them to work with small amounts of paint.
● Encourage older children to take prints of the patterns they make and experiment in moving their fingers around on the paper to spread the paint beneath it. What different patterns can they create?

Further activities
● Provide a selection of tools for the children to use to make patterns in the paint. These could include a variety of combs, hairbrushes, scrapers or patterned rollers.
● Help the children to squirt different colours of ready-mixed paint onto the table and mix them together with their fingers. Let them sprinkle dry powder paint or glitter onto the paints to achieve different effects.

Home link
Invite parents or carers to stay and observe a painting session and see the enjoyment their children get from using paint.

Cross-curricular links
Stepping Stones
● Engage in activities requiring hand-eye coordination. **(PD)**
● Demonstrate increasing skill and control in the use of mark-making implements, blocks, construction sets and 'small-world' activities. **(PD)**
Early Learning Goal
● Handle tools, objects, construction and malleable materials safely and with increasing control. **(PD)**

Early printing

The children are introduced to printing as they dip objects into paint and make marks on paper. They mix colours together and talk about what they have discovered.

What you need

Trays of ready-mixed paint; empty trays; assorted items to produce a variety of textures, such as: pastry cutters, wooden bricks, plastic bottles, lids, lollipop sticks and stickle bricks; paper of different textures, colours and sizes; aprons.

Early painters enjoy simple mark-making with objects found around the setting.
More confident painters mix colours and experiment in overprinting using a variety of objects.

Learning objectives
Stepping Stones
● Differentiate marks and movements on paper. **(CD)**
● Choose particular colours to use for a purpose. **(CD)**
● Talk about personal intentions, describing what they were trying to do. **(CD)**
Early Learning Goals
● Explore colour, texture, shape, form and space in two or three dimensions. **(CD)**
● Express and communicate their ideas, thoughts and feelings by using a widening range of materials. **(CD)**

What to do
● Set up a printing area with paint, empty trays, assorted items for printing and paper. Ask the children to name the colours of the paint. Tell them that you want them to make marks on the paper, using only the things they see on the table. What could they do?
● Ensure children put aprons on then work alongside them, encouraging them and showing them printing techniques. Let the children dip the objects into the paint, wipe off any excess on the side of the tray, and then press them firmly onto the paper. Show the children how to print on top of existing prints to produce different effects. Encourage them to talk about what they are doing
● Ask the children to choose two paint colours and pour them both into one tray. If they mix the colours together what will happen? Can they make a new colour?

Spend time mixing colours and talking about the colours they have made.
● The children could use the new colours they have created on their printed page. If they wish they could create a picture or pattern using this technique.

Support and extension
● Younger children may need extra support and encouragement in manoeuvring objects from the paint tray to paper.
● Older children can explore in more detail, overprinting with different shapes and colours.

Further activities
● Introduce different types of paint into the printing process, such as fluorescent, pearlised or metallic. Print onto textured or coloured paper.
● As a group project, print a length of fabric to use in a display as part of a cross-curricular theme. Purchased sponges or stampers with chunky handles, in the shape of animals, mathematical shapes or numbers, are ideal.

Home link
Invite the children to take home their work and talk to their parents and carers about what they have done.

Cross-curricular links
Stepping Stones
● Use one-handed tools and equipment. **(PD)**
● Demonstrate increasing skill and control in the use of mark-making implements, blocks, construction sets and 'small-world' activities. **(PD)**
Early Learning Goal
● Handle tools, objects, construction and malleable materials safely and with increasing control. **(PD)**

Dabbers and circles

In this activity, the children experiment in painting circles onto a large cardboard box using a variety of 'dabbers'. Then, they draw with thick black felt-tipped pens onto their design.

What you need

Collection of dabbers, made by tying objects such as sponges, scourers, bubble wrap or lint to sticks; purchased sponge dabbers; paper; ready-mixed powder paint in tubs; one large, plain cardboard box; aprons; thick black felt-tipped pens.

What to do

● Show the children the collection of dabbers and demonstrate how different effects can be achieved by dipping them into paint and dabbing them onto paper. Ask the children to suggest other ways the dabbers could be used to create a range of marks, for example, by using their sides or ends to draw broad or narrow lines. Put on aprons and let the children experiment with you and talk about the results.

● Draw a large circle in the air and ask the children what shape it is. Ask them to use their fingers to draw large and small circles in the air, on the table or on the floor. Show the children the large cardboard box and explain that you want them to use the dabbers to paint circles of all different sizes onto the sides of the box.

● Leave the box and paints out over several sessions, so that other children can also contribute to the painting. Gather the children together from time to time to look at the work in progress and talk about the shapes and colours. Encourage the children to experiment in painting

smaller circles inside larger ones, painting circles in the gaps or overlapping them.

● When the box is covered in painted circles, remove the paint and dabbers and introduce thick black felt-tipped pens. Give the children the freedom to draw onto the circle design. They may continue with the circle theme or incorporate lines, drawings, letters or patterns as they wish. Encourage the children to talk about their ideas and reflect upon what they have done.

Support and extension

● Younger children may find it easier to work on a large piece of paper on the floor rather than a box.

● Ask older children to choose a colour and shape theme for their box. They may like to use two or three boxes of different sizes, which they can display on top of one another.

Further activities

● Present the children with a selection of circles of different sizes cut out of black and white paper, tubs of black and white paint and dabbers. Ask them to use the dabbers to paint black designs on the white circles and white designs on the black circles. The children can then arrange the circles together to make one large design.

● Ask the children to use chalk to draw a circle on a path or play area. Provide a selection of dabbers and small buckets of water for them to experiment in mark-making inside the circles.

Play link

Encourage the children to find out about the properties of circles by providing a collection, including items, such as: hoops and wheels. They can try rolling them, fitting them together, placing one inside another or on top of each other. **(MD)**

Home link

Suggest that parents or carers encourage their children to be aware of shapes around them, by going on a 'circle hunt', either in the home or on the way to the setting.

Cross-curricular links
Stepping Stones
● Use talk to connect ideas, explain what is happening and anticipate what might happen next. **(CLL)**
● Draw lines and circles using gross motor movement. **(CLL)**
Early Learning Goals
● Use talk to organise, sequence and clarify thinking, ideas, feelings and events. **(CLL)**
● Use a pencil and hold it effectively to form recognisable letters, most of which are correctly formed. **(CLL)**

Welly walk

The children go out on a wet day in their wellington boots, splash in puddles and make muddy footprints. They examine the patterns on the soles of shoes and boots, and later make footprints by dipping their boots into paint and walking along paper pathways.

Early painters make random footprints in their wellington boots.
More confident painters experiment in making different patterns when making footprints.

What you need
Pair of old wellington boots for each child; collection of footwear, including: shoes, slippers, football boots, walking boots, tap and ballet shoes; dry area set up outside that includes brown paint in a large tray and pathways made from rolls of fairly thick paper, such as wallpaper; aprons.

What to do
● Ask the children to bring a pair of old wellington boots to leave in the setting until there is a wet day. When that day arrives, talk about the appropriate clothes they need to wear in wet weather and why waterproof boots are necessary. If possible, go for a walk in a wet, muddy area so that the children can enjoy splashing in the puddles

and making footprints in the mud. Encourage the children to think about what they are doing by posing questions, such as: *What will happen to the puddles when it stops raining and the Sun comes out?*
● When you are back in the setting and the boots are clean, ask the children to turn over their boots and compare the patterns on the soles. Do they know why the soles of the boots are patterned? Show the children the collection of footwear. After explaining that the patterned sole of a wellington boot helps to give grip on slippery ground, see if the children can explain why the slippers have a smooth sole.
● Go outside and show the

Learning objectives
Stepping Stones
● Differentiate marks and movements on paper. **(CD)**
● Work creatively on a large or small scale. **(CD)**
Early Learning Goal
● Explore colour, texture, shape, form and space in two or three dimensions. **(CD)**

children the tray of 'mud' and the pathways made from wallpaper. Put on aprons and ask them to dip each foot carefully in the paint in their wellington boots and then go for a walk, painting muddy footprints along the paper pathway. Ask the children to try and avoid any existing footprints on the path. When the paint has dried, the children can follow the footprints wearing their shoes.

Support and extension
● Younger children will need a helping hand when standing in the paint and walking along the footpath.
● Encourage older children to experiment in making different patterns with their feet, for example, making a single line of footprints by placing one foot directly in front of another, or they could make two lines of prints close together by 'shuffling' along.

Further activities
● Use the footprints as a stimulus for storytelling. Follow the footprints and ask the children to tell you where they were going, who they met along the way and what they saw.
● Provide ready-mixed paints and large sheets of paper. Ask the children to dip their

index and middle fingers into the paint and 'walk' around the paper pretending that they are small animals leaving their footprints. They can draw a picture of the animal at the beginning of the trail of prints and items such as trees along the way.

Play link
Ask the children if they think animals would leave footprints in mud, sand or snow. How would the animal footprints differ from their own footprints? Show the children pictures of animal footprints and ask them which animals they think would leave the largest and smallest prints. Provide a large tray of damp sand and some small-world animals, and let the children experiment in making animal tracks across the tray. **(KUW)**

Home link
Suggest that in warm weather parents or carers find a safe paved outdoor area and let their children dip their bare feet into a bowl of water and make footprints, noticing the way that the footprints disappear as the water evaporates.

Cross-curricular links
Stepping Stones
● Explore objects. **(KUW)**
● Notice and comment on patterns. **(KUW)**
Early Learning Goal
● Look closely at similarities, differences, patterns and change. **(KUW)**

Rolling around

In this activity, the children sort 3D shapes, picking out those that will roll. They cover tubes and balls in paint and roll these in a tray lined with paper, noticing the different marks made.

Early painters use toy rolling pins covered in paint to make marks.
More confident painters roll a variety of tubes in different coloured paints to make multicoloured marks on a sheet of paper.

What you need
Collection of 3D shapes, such as: recycled boxes, tubes of different sizes and small balls; trays with the bases covered thinly with different coloured paint; empty tray lined with paper; aprons.

What to do
● Show the children the collection of 3D shapes. Ask them to sort all of the shapes that will roll. Ask: *Why do these roll, but boxes do not? What is special about their sides?* Talk about the fact that all of the tubes are the same shape with curved sides, but they are different sizes. What shape can they see at each end of the tubes? Ask the children to look at the way in which the tubes roll and compare this with the way

the balls roll. If appropriate for the children, introduce the mathematical names of the shapes.
● Tell the children that you want them to use these shapes to make marks with paint. Put on aprons and show them the tray of paint and ask them if they can think of a way that they can use the tubes and balls to make marks. Let the children roll the tubes in paint and then onto the paper in the other tray.
● Next, ask them to roll a ball in a tray of a different coloured paint and then roll the ball into the tray containing the paper, moving the tray around so that the ball creates marks. Ask: *Do the tubes and balls make the same kind of*

Learning objectives
Stepping Stones
● Differentiate marks and movements on paper. **(CD)**
● Explore what happens when they mix colours. **(CD)**
Early Learning Goal
● Explore colour, texture, shape, form and space in two or three dimensions. **(CD)**

marks? *When one colour rolls on top of another, what happens?*

● Encourage the children to experiment by putting three or four balls in different coloured paints and rolling them around together at the same time in a tray lined with paper. Encourage the children to talk about the marks they have made and colours produced.

Support and extension
● Younger children may find it easier to roll toy rolling pins in paint and then roll the paint onto paper.
● Ask older children to use tubes of varying lengths, rolled in different coloured paints to create a variety of marks on one piece of paper.

Further activities
● Provide cardboard tubes or plastic piping cut into lengths, and items for the children to wind around the tubes, such as: thick rubber bands, hair scrunchies, textured yarn or string. Let the children experiment in mark-making as they roll the tubes in white

paint and then onto coloured paper.
● Show the children how to roll Plasticine or clay into a thick 'sausage' shape. Let them experiment in making indentations in the surface of their 'sausages' by pressing objects, such as pen tops, lollipop sticks or straws, into the modelling material. When dry, the children can sponge paint over their shapes and roll them onto paper.

Play link
Provide a box of balls of different sizes, assorted tubes and pieces of plastic piping for the children to play with and discover their properties. **(MD)**

Home link
Encourage parents or carers to help their children identify cylinders or 'tube shapes' at home. Such as tins and rolls of foil.

Cross-curricular links
Stepping Stones
● Show an interest in shape and space by playing with shapes or making arrangements with objects. **(MD)**
● Begin to use mathematical names for 'solid' 3D shapes and 'flat' 2D shapes and mathematical terms to describe shapes. **(MD)**
Early Learning Goal
● Use language such as 'circle' or 'bigger' to describe the shape and size of solids and flat shapes. **(MD)**

Herbs and washes

The children have the opportunity to use their senses as they examine inexpensive or home-grown herbs. They paint washes in the 'herb' colours, using a piece of the herb plant.

Early painters enjoy discovering the different smells of the herbs before painting with prepared washes.
More confident painters examine the plants and try to mix washes in colours to match the plants.

What you need

Collection of inexpensive or home-grown herbs, such as: mint, rosemary, parsley, thyme, lavender or basil; lavender-scented soap or bubble bath; digital camera; washes made in the colours of the herbs; paper; aprons.

What to do

● Before the start of this session, check with parents or carers that the children do not have any allergies to plants, scented soaps or bubble baths.
● Let the children touch and smell the herbs by giving them a piece of each plant. Encourage them to talk about and describe the smells they like and dislike and to ask questions. If you have an example of a lavender plant, show them a bar of lavender-scented soap or bubble bath and

ask if they can match the smell to the herb.
● Ask the children to look carefully at the colours, shapes and sizes of the leaves, and to compare and describe these. Take close-up photographs of each herb to use later. Break off a small piece of each herb and keep these for the children to match to the corresponding photographs later on.
● Put on aprons and show the children how to make a wash by mixing a small amount of paint with a large amount of water. Ask them to help you mix the colours of the herbs. Explain to the children that you want them to paint a herb garden by dipping pieces of the herbs into the wash and painting lines and marks onto paper. They should fill the paper

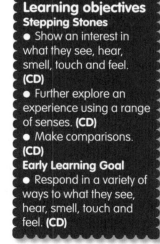

Learning objectives
Stepping Stones
● Show an interest in what they see, hear, smell, touch and feel. **(CD)**
● Further explore an experience using a range of senses. **(CD)**
● Make comparisons. **(CD)**
Early Learning Goal
● Respond in a variety of ways to what they see, hear, smell, touch and feel. **(CD)**

with areas of colour.

● When dry, display the children's finished pictures next to the photographs and pieces of herb you saved earlier. Can the children match the piece of herb to the correct photograph?

Support and extension

● Younger children may need to use ready-prepared washes for their painting.

● Invite older children to look closely at the different colours in the herb plants, and to mix their own coloured washes that they want to use to represent the colours of the herbs.

Further activities

● Make a herb garden together. This could be as small as two or three plant pots on a windowsill or as large as a bed in a sensory garden. Encourage the children to care for the plants and enjoy their smell as they are playing each day. Name the plants and ask the children to make labels that can be laminated and pushed into the plant pot or soil near the plants.

● Provide bottles of flavourings used in cooking, such as: vanilla, lemon,

peppermint, almond or ginger. Remind the children that these are for smelling only, not for tasting. Let the children smell the flavourings, close their eyes and tell you the colour they think of when they smell a particular flavouring. Can they give reasons for their choices? Discuss their ideas and decide together which colour to use for each particular smell. Mix the paint colour and add a few drops of the flavouring. Let the children smell and use their scented paints.

Play link

Provide a toy gardening set containing a trowel, fork, plant pots, plant catalogue, watering can, some artificial plants and compost to encourage role play and language development. **(CLL)**

Home link

Ask parents or carers to let their children look after a potted herb which they chose and bought.

Cross-curricular links
Stepping Stones
● Show curiosity, observe and manipulate objects. **(KUW)**
● Examine objects and living things to find out more about them. **(KUW)**
Early Learning Goal
● Investigate objects and materials by using all of their senses as appropriate. **(KUW)**

Foam painting

The children have the opportunity to make and discover the properties of different kinds of foam. They paint with foam, using their hands or spoons.

Early painters have fun painting with the coloured foam as they squirt, spoon and shape it.
More confident painters work together to make a large foam painting on a play surface outside.

What you need

Several bowls of shaving foam and foam made by whisking together a small amount of washing-up liquid, a small amount of water and drops of food colouring; spoons; icing bags; bowl of warm water for washing hands; soap; paper towels; aprons; digital camera.

What to do

● Before the start of this session, check with parents and carers for any allergies to shaving foam or washing-up liquid. If possible, choose a warm summer's day for this activity.
● Put on aprons and show the children the bowls of assorted foam and ask them to feel the texture of the foam, describing its appearance and smell. Ask the children if all of the foams feel the same and to describe any differences between them. Invite them to look closely at the foam made from washing-up liquid and water and ask if they can see that it is made from lots of bubbles.
● Add food colouring to the shaving foam. Encourage the children to explore the properties of the foam by standing it in peaks, blowing it, putting it on the palms of their hands and turning their hands over. Does the foam fall off? Can they change the shape of the foam?
● Tell the children that you want them to experiment in painting with the foam on any areas outside, such as the play surface, fence,

Learning objectives
Stepping Stones
● Begin to describe the texture of things. **(CD)**
● Work creatively on a large or small scale. **(CD)**
● Respond to comments and questions, entering into a dialogue about their creations. **(CD)**
Early Learning Goals
● Explore colour, texture, shape, form and space in two or three dimensions. **(CD)**
● Respond in a variety of ways to what they see, hear, touch and feel. **(CD)**

gate or wall. They could paint lines, dots, squiggles, shapes or faces, but instead of painting with brushes they will be using their hands, spoons or icing bags filled with foam.

● Ask the children to describe how using the foam differs from using paint. See if they can explain in simple terms that when they use paint the finished product is 2D, whereas their foam paintings are 3D. Take photographs of their work and, later in the day, ask the children to look at their work again to see if the foam has changed in shape. Can they speculate why?

● At the end of the session, ask the children to wash away the foam.

Support and extension

● Encourage younger children to enjoy the experience of spooning, squirting and shaping the foam.

● Invite older children to make a large foam painting together. Choose a theme to fit in with another area of the curriculum you are covering. For example: if your theme is 'My body', you could ask the children to paint a picture of a person.

Further activities

● Collect plastic food containers of varying sizes and turn them upside down. Ask the children to imagine that these are cakes and they are going to paint shaving foam icing over them.

● Provide cones made from card and let the children fill these with foam 'ice cream', decorating them with confetti and 'flakes' made from sticks.

Play link

Provide bowls of warm water, plastic bowls, whisks and washing-up liquid. Show the children how to make foam by putting a small amount of washing-up liquid and water in a small bowl and whisking it. Let them experiment with this. They should discover that the more they whisk, the larger the volume of foam they make. **(KUW)**

Home link

Suggest to parents and carers that they let their children experiment with the properties of foam at bathtime by adding bubble bath to the water and a collection of clean plastic containers to fill and empty.

Cross-curricular links
Stepping Stone
● Explore malleable materials by patting, stroking, poking, squeezing, pinching and twisting them. **(PD)**
Early Learning Goal
● Handle tools, objects, construction and malleable materials safely and with increasing control. **(PD)**

Coloured rain

The children go for a walk in the rain, observing the way water drips and makes puddles. They use diluted paint in plant sprayers to make coloured rain and experiment in mixing colours together to produce different coloured raindrops.

Early painters enjoy spraying paint and watching as the colours run and mix together to make raindrops.
More confident painters experiment in mixing the correct consistency of paint to use in the sprayers and decide the best way to position the paper to allow the raindrops to run down.

What you need

Wet-weather clothes; old towels; large sheets of paper to fasten to an easel or wall; small plant sprayers filled with water and some with 'coloured rain' (diluted with red, yellow, blue and white paint); aprons.

What to do

● Incorporate this activity into cross-curricular work about the weather. Watch raindrops running down a window together. Pose questions to encourage the children to think and be observant, for example: *Where does rain come from? Are all of the raindrops the same size? Which way do they travel?*

● Choose a rainy day and talk about the need to wear appropriate clothes for going outdoors when it is raining. Ensure that the children are all dressed for wet weather and then go for a walk. Look at the way in which rain settles on different surfaces, runs down window-panes, makes small puddles on windowsills and large puddles in dips and hollows in the road or path. Watch rain dripping from leaves, umbrellas or the ends of noses.

● When you are back in the setting, put towels on a windowsill and let the children spray water at the top of the window-pane and watch the 'rain' run down. Fix large sheets of paper to a wall or easel and show the children the

Learning objectives
Stepping Stone
● Explore what happens when they mix colours. **(CD)**
Early Learning Goal
● Explore colour, texture, shape, form and space in two or three dimensions. **(CD)**

sprayers filled with watery paint. Explain that it is paint, but for this activity they are going to pretend it is coloured rain. Ask the children to put on aprons and choose one colour and spray the 'rain' at the top of the piece of paper and watch how it moves, following the raindrops down the paper.

● Let the children experiment in spraying yellow rain on top of blue, yellow on red, or red on blue. What will happen when the different coloured rains mix together? What colour are the raindrops? Introduce a sprayer containing white rain. Encourage the children to speculate what will happen if they spray white on top of each of the colours. Give them time to experiment and talk about their findings. Include the finished work as part of a weather or colour display.

Support and extension

● Invite younger children to spray the paint randomly over the paper and watch how it runs and mixes together with other colours.
● Ask older children to decide how to position the paper to allow the paint to run down and mix their own 'rain' colours, discovering which consistency is best to produce very runny paint.

Further activities

● Wet a piece of absorbent paper using a damp sponge. Use eye-droppers to drip coloured 'rain' onto the paper and see how the colours mix together.
● Have a raindrop race. Two children spray water at the top of a window and see which drip reaches the bottom first. Time the drips with a stopwatch or by counting out loud.

Play link

Provide a water tray and items that will let water run or drip through them, such as watering cans, water wheels, sand sieves, eye-droppers and squeezy bottles. Let the children experiment in dripping water in different ways. **(KUW)**

Home link

Encourage parents or carers to involve their children in activities that include water at home, such as washing up, washing dolls, washing the car or using a hosepipe or sprinkler.

Cross-curricular links
Stepping Stone
● Use talk to connect ideas, explain what is happening and anticipate what might happen next. **(CLL)**
Early Learning Goal
● Use talk to organise, sequence and clarify thinking, ideas, feelings and events. **(CLL)**

Just my hands

In this activity, the children examine flowers using their senses before mixing scented paints and painting flower pictures, using different parts of their hands to make one large painting.

Early painters experience mark-making with scented paints.
More confident painters examine the colours and shapes of flowers and mix paints to match the colours of the flowers.

What you need

Flowers, including daisies; powder paints; margarine tubs; large sheet of green paper; fragrances, such as lavender or rose water; vase of flowers; collection of books about plants; aprons; hand-washing facilities.

What to do

● Before this lesson check for plant and perfume allergies. If possible, arrange a visit to a park or garden where there is a variety of scented flowers, including some that have petals radiating from the centre. Alternatively, bring a bunch of flowers into the setting. Ask the children to look at and describe the colours of the flowers, noticing if there are different shades of one colour. Ask them to smell the flowers and say which scent they like and why.

● Show the children the powder paint including red, yellow, blue and white. Ask them to put on aprons and choose one of the flowers and help you to mix a small quantity of thick paint in a margarine tub matching the colour of the flower. Use the colour mixing as an opportunity to use language, such as: 'add more', 'darker', 'lighter', 'shades of' and 'paler'. Make several pots of colour to paint the different flowers. Mix shades of green for the leaves.

● Let the children smell the different fragrances and

Learning objectives
Stepping Stones
● Differentiate marks and movements on paper. **(CD)**
● Explore what happens when they mix colours. **(CD)**
● Show an interest in what they see, hear, smell, touch and feel. **(CD)**
Early Learning Goals
● Explore colour, texture, shape, form and space in two or three dimensions. **(CD)**
● Respond in a variety of ways to what they see, hear, smell, touch and feel. **(CD)**

choose which one to add to each tub of paint, mixing well.

● Provide a large sheet of green paper, at least 1m², and encourage the children to work together on the same sheet painting 'daisy' type flowers, using only their hands. They could use the base of the fist to paint the centre, surrounded by marks made with the second joint of the finger, the side of the hand to paint the petals and fingertips or nails to make patterns on the petals.

● Once they have painted the petals, ask the children to paint leaves in different shades of green, again using their hands.

● Examine the finished painting together and encourage the children to talk about the ways in which they painted their flowers. Display the painting with a vase of flowers and a collection of books about plants.

Support and extension

● Pre-mix the scented paints for younger children. Let them experiment in mark-making using different parts of their hands.

● Invite older children to paint their scented flowers onto card, cut out the flowers, tape them to sticks and stand them in a vase.

Further activities

● As a Christmas activity, ask the children to use their hands to paint Christmas trees using white paint on a dark background and their fingertips to add snow falling. Add silver glitter to make the trees sparkle.

● Using play dough, encourage the children to experiment in making as many different marks in it as they can, using different parts of their hands.

Play link

Provide a basket of resources such as books, CDs and puppets to encourage children to learn and enjoy finger rhymes such as 'Tommy Thumb'. **(CLL)**

Home link

Suggest that members of a family compare the sizes of their hands. The child can then draw around the hands of each member of their family, and cut out the hand shapes.

Cross-curricular links

Stepping Stones
● Have a positive approach to new experiences. **(PSED)**
● Display high levels of involvement in activities. **(PSED)**

Early Learning Goal
● Continue to be interested, excited and motivated to learn. **(PSED)**

Reasons for painting

House painters

The children become house painters and mix their own thick, textured paint using sand and glue, which they apply using spatulas to cover the cracks in a wall.

What you need
Pots of ready-mixed paints of varying colours; sand; glue; spoons and spatulas; picture of the outline of a house with several superficial cracks in the wall, drawn onto a large piece of paper; sticky label badges with 'House painter' written on them; aprons; washing-up facilities.

What to do
● Tell the children that they are going to be house painters and they have an important job to do. Show them the drawing of the house and point out the cracks. Explain that the owner of the house would like her house painted in several different colours, but she does not like the cracks in the wall and wants them covered with paint. As ordinary paint will not cover these cracks, it is their job as house painters to make a thick paint that will.
● Give each child their 'House painter' badge. Put the ready-mixed paints on a table and gather the children around you. Ask them to put on aprons and stir the paints and let the paint drip from the spoons, describing the consistency as they do so. Show the

Learning objectives
Stepping Stone
● Experiment to create different textures. **(CD)**
Early Learning Goal
● Explore colour, texture, shape, form and space in two or three dimensions. **(CD)**

children the glue and sand and ask them to speculate how the paint will be altered if these are added to it.

● Invite a child to add a spoonful of glue and a spoonful of sand to the paint, mixing it well. Talk about the way in which the paint has changed, how it feels or looks different as it is being stirred or dripped from a spoon. Pass the tub around the group, encouraging the children to discuss and describe the changes and speculate what will happen if they add more sand and glue to the paint. Repeat the process until the paint is of a thick consistency that can be applied using a spatula.

● Show the children a variety of spatulas and ask them to experiment in using these to apply the paint to the house wall, making sure that all of the cracks are covered. When the paint is dry, encourage the children to feel the texture and compare it to an ordinary painting. Ask the painters to wash and clean their paint pots and utensils ready for the next day's work.

Support and extension

● Younger children can simply enjoy the experience as they change the texture of the paint by adding sand and glue. They can spoon the textured paint onto paper.

● Invite older children to apply the textured paint to a large cardboard box (the house) and create patterns in the paint by using the end of a spatula.

Further activities

● Experiment in mixing and applying other textured 'wall' paints by replacing sand with fine grit, sawdust or salt. Compare the different textures when the paints are dry.

● Provide dry sand in the sand tray and watering cans filled with water. Ask the children to add water to the sand, noticing changes to the consistency until they achieve a consistency that they can mould into shapes. If they add more water, what happens?

Play link

Talk about the way that plasterers and bricklayers use sand, concrete and plaster to carry out their work. Create a role-play area that includes plastic bricks, sand, water, buckets, trowels, spatulas and spreaders to encourage the children to mix sand and water and to use 'spreading' movements when 'cementing' their bricks together. **(PD)**

Home link

Invite parents and carers to let their children experience mixing and spreading foods of different consistencies, such as jam, honey or peanut butter, as part of their day-to-day activities.

Cross-curricular links

Stepping Stones
● Use one-handed tools and equipment. **(PD)**
● Manipulate materials to achieve a planned effect. **(PD)**

Early Learning Goal
● Handle tools, objects, construction and malleable materials safely and with increasing control. **(PD)**

Ice blocks

This activity is ideal for a hot summer's day or an icy winter's day. The children experience the properties of ice and 'paint' pictures using ice cubes as blocks of colour.

Early painters 'paint' patterns or pictures using prepared ice cubes.
More confident painters choose the colours they want to freeze and 'paint' patterns based on a particular shape.

What you need

Use of a freezer; ice cubes; ice-cube trays and bags; small plastic containers; food colouring; ready-mixed paint; plastic cups; water; digital camera.

What to do

● Pour the children a cup of cold water each and ask them to take a sip. Is it hot or cold? How could they make it even colder? They may suggest putting it in the refrigerator or outside if it is a frosty day. Say that you could add ice and ask: *What is ice? How can you make it?* Talk about the way that puddles freeze on a very cold day or water freezes when put into a freezer.

● If it is an icy day, go outside and look at examples of ice. Put some ice cubes into the cups of water and ask the children to take another sip and see if it is any colder.

● Tell the children that you want them to make some ice. What do they need? Suggest that, as well as making ice in ice-cube trays or bags, they could try making it in different containers. Ask them to look around the setting for suitable items, remembering that the containers must be able to hold water. Add food colouring to water, fill the containers and freeze. Explain to the children that this ice is not for eating.

● Stress to the children that they should never touch ice cubes that have come immediately out of the freezer. Take the containers out of the freezer and watch as the ice shapes melt. How could the children make them melt more quickly? Point out that the water changed into ice and back to water again.

● Colour some more water with food colouring or paint

Learning objectives
Stepping Stones
● Show an interest in what they see, hear, smell, touch and feel. **(CD)**
● Further explore an experience using a range of senses. **(CD)**
Early Learning Goal
● Respond in a variety of ways to what they see, hear, smell, touch and feel. **(CD)**

and freeze different colours in several ice-cube trays. When frozen, put the ice cubes in a bowl and ask the children to 'paint' a pattern or picture using the ice cubes as blocks of colour. What are the ice colours like? What will happen to their work? Take photographs as a record.

Support and extension
● Encourage younger children to enjoy the texture of the ice cubes and arrange the ice colours freely to make a picture.
● Invite older children to choose the colours to make their ice shapes and 'paint' patterns based on a particular shape such as a circle or square.

Further activities
● Provide items, such as: sequins, small animal figures, beads and buttons. Ask the children to make a 3D ice picture by choosing items to put into a small plastic container, fill with water and freeze.
● Make small ice cubes coloured with paint. Arrange a few of them on a piece of

paper in a tray. When the ice has melted, what is left behind? The children can mix the colours and make patterns with their fingers. When the paint is dry, provide the children with felt-tipped pens and ask them to make the shapes into ice patterns or pictures.

Play link
Freeze a collection of objects filled with water, such as medical gloves, balloons and moulds. Fill the water tray with coloured water and add the ice shapes. Ask the children to predict what will happen to the ice as they play with it. Will it still be there the next day? **(KUW)**

Home link
Suggest that parents and carers help their children to make lollipops made from fruit juice.

Cross-curricular links
Stepping Stones
● Explore objects. **(KUW)**
● Talk about what is seen and what is happening. **(KUW)**
● Show an awareness of change. **(KUW)**
Early Learning Goal
● Look closely at similarities, differences, patterns and change. **(KUW)**

Magic paint

The practitioner sets a magical scene in this activity as the children mix colours and use a variety of ingredients to make 'magic paints' that they apply to paper with magic wands.

What you need

Labelled tubs containing powder paint and ready-mixed paint in red, yellow, blue and white; tubs containing 'lumps and bumps' (beads and glue mixed together), 'rainbow drops' (shiny confetti); shakers containing 'magic dust' (gold glitter) and 'starlight' (silver glitter); mixing bowls; large and small spoons; sparkly ribbon; shiny box containing the 'Magic paint recipes' on photocopiable page 28, cut out and mounted on shiny paper; 'wands' made from pieces of dowelling or cane with short lengths of silver gift ribbon tied to the ends; photocopiable page 29 'Star shapes'; glue; paper.

What to do

● The preparation of resources and the way you set the scene is an important aspect of this activity. In order to create the 'magic' feel, the materials need to look special, intriguing and different from everyday painting in order to capture the children's imaginations.

● Prepare and label the tubs of 'magic ingredients' and display them attractively together. Mount the magic paint recipes on to shiny paper, put in a special box and tie with a sparkly ribbon. Gather the

children around you and show them the box and magic ingredients. Explain that you found these things on the table when you came into the setting that morning, but you do not know where they could have come from. Who could have put them there? Talk about the fact that they look very different and exciting. Read the labels on the magic ingredients together and encourage the children to speculate about what might be in the box as the suspense builds.

● Open the box with some drama to reveal the magic paint recipes. Read these together and ask the children if they would like to try out the recipes using the ingredients. Maintain the excitement as you mix the ingredients together. Encourage the children to discuss what will happen as you add the different colours, and let them apply the paints to paper, using the wands.

● Ask the children to experiment in creating their own recipes using three or four ingredients, either you or they can record these on the stars provided on photocopiable page 29 'Star shapes'. Add a blob of the new magic paint next to the recipe. Talk about the colours and textures of paint they have made. Ask the children to think of names for their magic paint recipes and add them to the box for others to use.

Support and extension
● Younger children need not use the recipes and can enjoy experimenting freely as they mix the ingredients together.
● Encourage older children to suggest extra ingredients to add to the collection to make different kinds of magic paint.

Further activities
● Use eye-droppers to take small amounts of vibrantly coloured inks to mix to create magic ink recipes.
● Put the magic paint or ink recipes together in a special book. Cover with silver paper and display with a silver wand for the children to use as they read the book.

Play link
Encourage imaginative play by providing a box of magic wands, magic dust (glitter), shiny or glittery fabrics and fairy or wizard costumes if available. **(CD)**

Home link
Parents and carers could involve their children when they are mixing ingredients or following a recipe.

Cross-curricular links
Stepping Stone
● Display high levels of involvement in activities. **(PSED)**
Early Learning Goal
● Be confident to try new activities, initiate ideas and speak in a familiar group. **(PSED)**

Magic paint recipes

Orange sunshine
Mix:
- A blob of yellow
- A big shake of red
- A spoonful of magic dust

Purple shimmer
Mix:
- A big blob of blue
- A small blob of red
- A shake of rainbow drops

Green frog
Mix:
- A big spoonful of yellow
- A teaspoonful of blue
- A handful of lumps and bumps

Sparkle
Mix:
- Two blobs of white
- A spoonful of glue
- Two shakes of starlight

Star shapes

SCHOLASTIC
www.scholastic.co.uk

Grand prix

This activity is best undertaken outdoors, as it involves making a racetrack with wet plaster bandage. The children paint the track using sponges, rollers and cotton buds.

Early painters experience using different materials to shape and mould a surface that they paint with sponges.
More confident painters overprint the scenery using sponges to give a more textured finish.

What you need
Large piece of hardboard or strong cardboard; newspapers; plaster bandage; bowl of water; powder paints; plastic tubs; sponges; narrow rollers or cotton buds; modelling material; chalk; cones; few chairs; plastic tools; pretend walkie-talkies; selection of ride-on toys; toy cars.

What to do
● Make a car racetrack outside that is big enough to take ride-on outdoor toys, by drawing the track outline with chalk and adding cones around the edge. Draw a 'pit stop' area and add a few chairs on one side for the grandstand. Put a box of plastic tools and walkie-talkies in the pit stop. For safety reasons, the activity should be well supervised to ensure that children enjoy driving around the track safely on ride-on toys.

● After they have used the track, suggest to the children that, as they enjoyed it so much, they might like to make a track to use with their toy cars. Discuss the shape they want the track to be. Do they want it to have bends and hills? Use a large piece of hardboard for the base and ask the children to help build the hills for the track, using upturned plastic tubs, yoghurt pots and damp newspaper. Place and smooth layers of wet plaster bandage over the newspaper until you have a hilly 'landscape'. Ask the children to describe what the wet plaster bandage

Learning objectives
Stepping Stones
● Make three-dimensional structures. **(CD)**
● Begin to describe the texture of things. **(CD)**
● Understand that different media can be combined. **(CD)**
Early Learning Goal
● Explore colour, texture, shape, form and space in two or three dimensions. **(CD)**

feels like. Do they like the texture? Does it feel like anything else they have ever touched?

● When the landscape is dry, you can decide together how to paint it. The children will need to make some decisions. Support them by asking questions, such as: *Where is the racetrack – in the desert, in the countryside or near to the sea?* When they have decided on the location, they can decide which colours they should use to paint the landscape. Help them to mix the appropriate colours using powder paint. Apply the paints using small pieces of sponge.

● Draw the road using narrow rollers or cotton buds dipped in black paint. When the paint is dry, make 'START' and 'FINISH' signs, fixing them in place with modelling material. The track is then ready for the cars to practise before the race.

Support and extension
● Younger children will need help in constructing the track, but can enjoy applying the wet plaster bandage.
● Ask older children to overprint in different colours with sponges to add depth and colour to the landscape.

Further activities
● Add small-world scenery to the racetrack. Create flags from triangles of coloured paper glued to lollipop sticks pushed into modelling material and arrange these around the length of the track.
● Make figures from modelling material or pipe-cleaners and place them at the side of the track as spectators.

Play link
Set up an area with cardboard boxes of various sizes, thick felt-tipped pens and a good selection of toy cars so that the children can make items such as garages or car show rooms and use these in imaginative play. **(CD)**

Home link
Suggest that parents and carers encourage their children to be observant and take an interest in the world around them, by talking about the different types of cars they see.

Cross-curricular links
Stepping Stones
● Explore malleable materials by patting, stroking, poking, squeezing, pinching and twisting them. **(PD)**
● Manipulate materials to achieve a planned effect. **(PD)**
Early Learning Goal
● Handle tools, objects, construction and malleable materials safely and with increasing control. **(PD)**

Bricklayers

In this activity, the children become bricklayers. They first look at buildings in their environment and then use paint to print textured bricks to make walls, which they later use to make a role-play building site.

Early painters make marks with wooden blocks covered in different textured materials.

More confident painters look at patterns used in laying bricks and experiment in printing their own textured brick patterns.

What you need

Collection of different coloured and textured building bricks; large cardboard boxes; paper; 'play' hard hats; builders' fluorescent vests; collection of rectangular objects for printing, such as scouring pads; wooden blocks covered with textured materials, such as: pieces of foam, bubble wrap, corrugated card or string (wound around the block); tubs of brick-coloured paints; digital camera; aprons.

What to do

● Show the children the collection of assorted building bricks and ask them to describe their shape, colour and texture. The children should only handle bricks under close supervision. Ask the children when bricks are used and talk about the different types of buildings that could be made from brick. Ask if they know whose job it is to lay bricks and explain that they are going to be bricklayers for a day.

● Give the children hard hats and builders' vests. Explain that as trainee bricklayers they will need to look at a variety of walls and buildings to get some ideas before starting work.

● Go for a walk around the local environment, asking the children to identify different types of buildings, such as: houses, flats, shops and churches. Let them touch walls, noticing the textures, colours and patterns of the bricks. Ask the children to tell you what is holding the bricks together. Talk about the fact that the bricklayers lay

Learning objectives
Stepping Stone
● Experiment to create different textures. **(CD)**
Early Learning Goal
● Explore colour, texture, shape, form and space in two or three dimensions. **(CD)**

bricks in straight rows with mortar holding them together. Take close-up photographs of bricks laid in different patterns for the children to refer to later.

● Back in the setting, exchange the vests for aprons and ask the children to use the rectangular-shaped blocks covered with different textured materials to print walls by dipping the blocks into paint. Scrape off excess paint on the side of the pot and press the blocks onto the sides of cardboard boxes or large sheets of paper to make rows of bricks. Talk with the children about their work, asking them to compare the textured effects they have created. When dry, the printed boxes and 'walls' can form the basis of a role-play building site.

Support and extension

● Younger children can enjoy the experience of mark-making using the wooden blocks and talk about the different textures they have created.

● Invite older children to experiment in 'laying' their bricks in different patterns.

Further activities

● Devote a large space to making a building site role-play area. Include the children's printed boxes and add cardboard tubes for them to use to construct buildings.

Make a site office with telephone, computer, pens and paper to encourage speaking and listening, and writing skills. Remind the children that they should never go into a real building site.

● Give the children the opportunity to experiment in building walls in different patterns by providing a wheelbarrow full of wooden bricks, spreaders, and laminated photographs of brick patterns. Can they suggest a way of sticking the bricks together?

Play link

Provide construction sets and pictures of different types of buildings to encourage the children to experiment in making a range of buildings that they see in their local environment on the way to the setting. **(KUW)**

Home link

Suggest that parents and carers talk to their children about the type of building in which they live, naming and counting the different rooms.

Cross-curricular links

Stepping Stones
● Demonstrate increasing skill and control in the use of mark-making implements, blocks, construction sets and 'small-world' activities. **(PD)**
● Notice differences between features of the local environment. **(KUW)**
Early Learning Goals
● Handle tools, objects, construction and malleable materials safely and with increasing control. **(PD)**
● Observe, find out about and identify features in the place they live and the natural world. **(KUW)**

Fish puppets

This activity can be linked to a pet, underwater or animal theme. The children use their handprints to make fish puppets, which they decorate with sequins and glitter.

Early painters make handprints and create their puppets with adult support.
More confident painters make decisions about the shape of their fish, cutting out and mounting their puppets themselves.

What you need

Ready-mixed powder paints in shallow trays; brightly coloured card; paper; glitter; sequins; thread; scissors; glue; cotton buds; green yarns; ribbons; strips of tissue paper or Cellophane; sticks or lengths of cane; pens or crayons; fish or books about fish; finger-paints.

What to do

● Check if any children have allergies to paint. If possible, let the children see fish swimming in a tank. Alternatively, use books or the internet as sources of pictures. Ask the children to look carefully at the fins and tails of the fish, and the way they move. Show the children how they can use their hands as imaginary fish, with their fingers as the tail and thumb as a fin. Demonstrate by drawing a fish's eye and mouth on your hand using finger-paint. Ask the children to let their 'fish' swim, glide and dart. Show them how to alter the shape of the tails of their fish by opening or closing their fingers.

● Tell the children that you want them to make fish puppets by making their hands into the shape of a fish, and pressing the palms of their hands into paint to make a handprint on a piece of paper. When dry, cut out the fish, mount on brightly coloured card and cut around the fish shape again. The children can add features using pens or crayons. Ask them to suggest how they can make the fish look wet. Encourage them to add glitter and sequins using cotton buds to apply the glue.

● Hang the fish from sticks using thread. Suggest that the children choose from a selection of green yarns,

Learning objectives
Stepping Stone
● Make constructions, collages, paintings, drawings and dances. **(CD)**
Early Learning Goal
● Explore colour, texture, shape, form and space in two or three dimensions. **(CD)**

ribbons, strips of tissue paper or Cellophane to make reeds and attach them to the stick.

Support and extension

● Younger children may need support in making their handprints. Cut out and mount the fish onto card for them.

● Older children can cut out and mount the fish themselves. Ask them to think about the shape and other materials they could use for decoration.

Further activities

● Make a fish tank to use for a puppet show by cutting a 'window' in one side of a large cardboard box and removing the flaps from the top. Show the children how to sponge print the inside and outside of the box in 'watery' colours. Ask them to select sand, shells and stones and place these in the bottom of the 'tank'. The children can then hold their sticks over the box so that the fish dangle and swim inside the tank.

● Talk to the children about keeping fish as pets and what fish need to keep healthy. Share books about pets and learn this poem from *A Yellow Poetry Paintbox* chosen by John Foster (Oxford University Press).

My Goldfish

My goldfish is
  the perfect pet
She isn't any trouble.
She doesn't bark.
She doesn't mew,
  just bubbles,
    bubbles,
      bubbles.

My goldfish is
  the perfect pet.
She isn't any trouble,
We don't have
  to feed her much.
She doesn't need
  a rabbit hutch,
    just bubbles,
      bubbles,
        bubbles.

By Marie Brookes

Play link

Involve the children in creating a simple underwater role-play area by hanging long strips of blue, green and white crêpe paper and Cellophane from the ceiling. Play 'watery' music to encourage imaginative play and movement. **(CD)**

Home link

Invite parents or carers to stay for a few minutes to watch as their children make their fish puppets 'swim' in the tank.

Cross-curricular links

Stepping Stone
● Construct with a purpose in mind, using a variety of resources. **(KUW)**

Early Learning Goal
● Select the tools and techniques they need to shape, assemble and join materials they are using. **(KUW)**

Detectives

The children become 'plant detectives', looking closely at leaves for seasonal changes and becoming aware of symmetry, as they draw and paint the missing half of a leaf. This activity is ideal for use in spring or autumn.

Early painters match colours and shapes as they paint their leaves.
More confident painters become aware of symmetry while they observe closely the shape, colours and the pattern of veins as they draw the missing half of the leaf.

What you need

Cardboard box labelled 'Detectives', containing magnifiers, notebooks (labelled 'Clues'), pencils, 'Detective' badges; digital camera; envelope labelled 'Leaves', containing pictures of large leaves, with one half of each leaf missing; wax crayons; oil pastels; washes; tissues or cotton wool.

What to do

● Tell the children that today they are going to be detectives, particularly looking at plants. This means they will be looking for clues about changes to plants and trees now that it is spring (or autumn). Show them the 'Detectives' box and ask them to speculate about what might be inside. Reveal the contents and give each child their 'Detective' badge and a magnifier. Show the children how to use the magnifiers and ask them to describe how things appear when they look through them.

● Go out into the local area and ask the children to look for any clues to changes in the trees or plants, using their magnifiers to help them. Take photographs of evidence. Are there new leaves? Have leaves changed colour? Have leaves fallen from trees? Use the magnifiers to examine both sides of leaves, noticing their shapes, colours and veins.

Learning objectives
Stepping Stone
● Show an interest in what they see, hear, smell, touch and feel. **(CD)**
Early Learning Goal
● Respond in a variety of ways to what they see, hear, smell, touch and feel. **(CD)**

Encourage the children to describe and write their observations in the 'Clues' notebook.

● After gathering clues, return to the setting and tell the children that you have some beautiful pictures of leaves to show them. Open the 'Leaves' envelope and feign shock to find that the leaves have been cut in half and half of each one has disappeared. What could that have happened? Has somebody taken them? Can the children help repair the leaves?

● Tell the children that you have an idea that might work. Ask them to take a leaf picture each and examine it carefully. Could they possibly draw the missing half of the leaf and colour it to match the piece that is left? Provide wax crayons, oil pastels and washes for the children to apply with tissues or cotton wool when creating the missing halves. Ask them to look at the effects they achieve. What happens when they dab a wash over the crayons and oil pastels? Cut out and display the completed leaves and congratulate the detectives on their hard work.

Support and extension

● Supply younger children with the missing half of the leaf drawing for them to colour with paint and crayons.

● Encourage older children to become aware of symmetry. Ask them to search around the setting for examples of symmetrical patterns or objects.

Further activities

● Discuss the changes the children can see in the environment as the seasons alter. Encourage the children to ask questions and help them to find the answers using information books.

● Let the children use the paint techniques from the main activity to create other things they saw when they were being detectives, such as flowers or birds.

Play link

Set up a 'nature detectives' area. Include small boxes of natural objects, such as fir cones, shells, seed heads and dried grasses, for the children to examine using magnifiers. Include paper, pencils and coloured pencils to encourage the children to record and sketch their findings. **(KUW)**

Home link

Invite parents and carers to play 'I spy' on the way to and from the setting, looking out for any seasonal changes.

Cross-curricular links
Stepping Stones
● Show awareness of symmetry. **(MD)**
● Describe simple features of objects and events. **(KUW)**
Early Learning Goals
● Talk about, recognise and recreate simple patterns. **(MD)**
● Find out about, and identify, some features of living things, objects and events they observe. **(KUW)**

Camouflage

This activity can be incorporated into cross-curricular work about animals. The children look at the camouflage colours and patterns found on animals' skin and fur that make them hard to see or help them blend into their surroundings. They use their fingers to paint patterns to 'hide' an animal in its surroundings.

Early painters work together to hide their animal shapes in the background, using random marks in their chosen colours.

More confident painters provide their own animals shapes and refer to pictures of animals to base their patterns on those they observe on an animal's skin or fur.

What you need
Pictures of animals that use camouflage, such as: tiger, zebra, cheetah, snake, crocodile; simple paper outlines of these animals; ready-mixed powder paints or finger-paints in the appropriate fur or skin colours; white tack; paper; pieces from a construction kit or small-world items.

What to do
● Before the session check if any children have allergies to powder paint. Show the children the pictures of animals that use camouflage. Talk about the fact that the animals may want to hide, so they are not seen by other animals that want to eat them, or they may be the hunter, hiding

from the animals they are trying to catch. Ask the children to describe the patterns and colours of the animals' coats or skins.
● Give each child a piece from a construction kit or small-world item and ask them to search around the setting until they find something else in the matching colour on which to place their object, to 'hide' it.
● Tell the children that you have some animals that you want them to hide so that other animals cannot see them. Show them the cut-out animal shapes and the pictures of each

Learning objectives
Stepping Stones
● Differentiate marks and movements on paper. **(CD)**
● Choose particular colours to use for a purpose. **(CD)**
● Respond to comments and questions, entering into dialogue about their creations. **(CD)**
Early Learning Goals
● Explore colour, texture, shape, form and space in two or three dimensions. **(CD)**
● Express and communicate their ideas, thoughts and feelings by using a widening range of materials. **(CD)**

particular animal. Talk about the colours and patterns on the animals' skin or fur. Ask the children to use white tack to fix their animal outline on a piece of paper and then refer to the animal pictures and choose the colours they need to paint their animals. They can use their fingers to dab, streak or smear the paint over the animal shape and entire piece of paper to recreate the camouflage pattern.

● When the paper is covered, let the children carefully remove the animal shape to reveal the white silhouette beneath it. Display the paintings and give the children time to enjoy matching the animals to their backgrounds.

Support and extension

● Invite younger children to work on a large scale together, painting just one animal such as a zebra, using narrow rollers to make the stripes.

● Ask older children to draw and cut out their own animal shapes to use in their pictures.

Further activities

● Provide a collection of fabric scraps, yarns, coloured papers, coloured pencils and crayons. Glue a small square of fake fur fabric to a piece of cartridge paper. Ask the children to look carefully at the fur fabric and find matching coloured materials and stick these to the paper to create their own piece of 'fur'.

● Show the children a collection of small-world animals and suggest that they make environments for them, using twigs, leaves and so on, either inside the setting or outside in a safe area.

Play link

Encourage imaginative play by providing props that the children can use to dress up as animals. These could include lengths of fabric, hatbands with animal faces, ears or horns attached, or ready-made animal costumes. Play 'Hide-and-seek' and catching games in the outdoor play area. **(CD)**

Home link

Invite parents and carers to see the children's artwork. Suggest they continue the theme by reading animal stories with their children.

Cross-curricular links
Stepping Stone
● Notice and comment on patterns. **(KUW)**
Early Learning Goal
● Look closely at similarities, differences, patterns and change. **(KUW)**

Spirals

Children learn about, draw and form spirals. They make spirals from Plasticine and use these to dip into paint and make patterns.

What you need
Collection of objects that incorporate spirals in their design; Plasticine or other malleable material; shallow trays filled with different coloured ready-mixed paints; piece of thick cardboard or hardboard; glue; pictures of snails; copies of photocopiable page 41 'Spiral shapes' enlarged to A3; paper.

Early painters coil lengths of Plasticine into spirals and print with adult support.
More confident painters print their spiral patterns and draw features to make the spirals into snails.

Learning objectives
Stepping Stone
● Make constructions, collages, paintings, drawings and dances. **(CD)**
Early Learning Goal
● Explore colour, texture, shape, form and space in two or three dimensions. **(CD)**

What to do
● Show the children the collection of objects that incorporate spirals in their design. Then, let the children trace the spirals on the photocopiable sheet with their fingers, noticing that a spiral is made from only one line. Ask them to think of a very small animal that has a spiral on its shell. If possible, go outside on a rainy day to look at real snails, or simply use pictures.
● Tell the children that you want them to make a spiral together. Ask them to join hands in a line and make a circle. Lead them round and round, making a spiral shape. When you are in the middle of the spiral, turn round and 'unwind' the spiral.
● Give the children a piece of Plasticine each and show them how to roll it out into a long 'sausage' shape. Ask them to try and make the 'sausage' into a spiral that they can hold in one hand. Then, ask the children to use their spirals to paint a picture by dipping them into the paint and pressing them onto paper. Encourage the children to fill the paper with coloured

spirals and then overprint.
● Ask the children to dip their spirals into paint once more and leave these to dry. Use the plasticine spirals to make a 3D design by arranging them closely together on a piece of hardboard or thick cardboard. Stick them into place and display.

Support and extension
● Provide younger children with the Plasticine already rolled into 'sausage' shapes and help them coil it into spirals.
● Invite older children to turn their spiral prints into snails by drawing the snail's body using oil pastels.

Further activities
● Make 'snail breads' using a bread mix, and let the children make spirals as they did in the main activity. Bake the dough and talk about the changes they notice.
● Find a safe area where snails can be found for the children to observe. Find information about snails using books, CD-ROMs or the internet.

Play link
Cover the photocopiable sheets with tracing paper and ask the children to trace over the spirals with thick pens as a pre-writing activity. **(CLL)**

Home link
Let the children take their pictures home to prompt talk about their day with their parents and carers.

Cross-curricular links
Stepping Stone
● Manipulate materials to achieve a planned effect. **(PD)**
Early Learning Goal
● Handle tools, objects, construction and malleable materials safely and with increasing control. **(PD)**

Spiral shapes

Paint sticks

In this activity the children pretend that there are no brushes in the setting, so they make their own 'paint sticks' from natural materials found on a walk. They experiment in making marks with their different textured paint sticks.

Early painters collect materials that the practitioner makes into paint sticks for them to use.
More confident painters work cooperatively with a partner to make their own paint sticks.

What you need

Safe outdoor area; paintbrushes of different sizes and shapes; pots of paint in 'earthy' colours; rubber bands; dowelling; string; sticky tape; natural materials, such as: leaves, seed heads, grasses, twigs, pieces of bark or flowers; paper.

What to do

● Display the collection of brushes in different sizes and shapes, including broad household paintbrushes. Ask the children what they think is used to make the handles and bristles of the brushes. See if they notice any difference in the 'feel' between the animal hair and nylon brushes.
● Tell the children that you want them to pretend that they are in a setting that has no paintbrushes at all. Every single one has

been lost and they have no money to buy any more. Could they make their own brushes or paint sticks? What would they need?
● Suggest that they start by going for a walk outside looking for items they could use to make their paint sticks. Check first that the children do not have any allergies to plants. Ask the children to look for materials to make the handles and 'bristles'. They can collect fallen twigs, leaves, daisies, seed heads, pieces of bark and grasses. Remind them that they should only pick up objects that have fallen to the ground naturally, and not pick or break off any flowers, leaves or branches.

Learning objectives
Stepping Stones
● Begin to describe the texture of things. **(CD)**
● Use available resources to create props to support role play. **(CD)**
Early Learning Goals
● Explore colour, texture, shape, form and space in two or three dimensions. **(CD)**
● Use their imagination in art and design, music, dance, imaginative and role play and stories. **(CD)**

Reasons for painting

● Encourage the children to feel and describe the textures of the materials and select the ones they want to use to make the bristles of their paint sticks. Using dowelling or twigs as handles, help the children attach the 'bristles' using rubber bands, tape or string. Discuss the different textures of the paint sticks they have made and ask the children to speculate about the marks they might make when the paint sticks are dipped in paint. Give the children time to experiment in making marks in earthy colours and display the paint sticks next to the finished paintings. Make sure that the children wash their hands after handling any found materials.

Support and extension
● Younger children can collect items on a walk to be made into paint sticks for them to use.
● Invite older children to work together with a partner making a set of their own paint sticks.

Further activities
● Suggest that the children choose a small-world wild animal, such as a hedgehog or mouse, that they could have seen on their walk. Ask them to paint a piece of paper using their paint sticks and cut it into pieces to cover a box to make a home for that animal. Add a notice outside each home, saying, 'Who lives here?'
● Make paint sticks from man-made materials, such as: plastic laces, paper clips joined together, strips of fabric or nylon yarn. Fasten these to the handles of plastic spoons.

Play link
Provide an assortment of natural and man-made materials, tubs of paint and assorted papers and boxes to encourage the children to experiment freely in mark-making. **(CD)**

Home link
Suggest parents and carers encourage their children to take an interest in their environment by noticing and talking about plants and animals they see around them.

Cross-curricular links
Stepping Stone
● Construct with a purpose in mind, using a variety of resources. **(KUW)**
Early Learning Goal
● Select the tools and techniques they need to shape, assemble and join materials they are using. **(KUW)**

Who lives here?

Painting and dancing

Music, dancing and painting become one in this activity as the children are free to move, dance and paint, in response to music.

Early painters are encouraged to respond to music and paint using sponges.
More confident painters mix the colours they want to use in response to the music.

What you need

Recording of a piece of lively dance music with a strong beat (for example, 'In the Mood' by Glen Miller); music player; ready-mixed powder paint in tubs; large sheets of paper, sponges; aprons.

What to do

● Clear a large space inside or outside and fasten large sheets of paper at child height, to boards, a fence or easels. Mix powder paint in tubs in a variety of colours and provide a selection of sponges.
● Play the music and ask the children what it makes them feel like doing. Let them move freely to the music. Encourage them to join you and any other adults present in dancing to the music, being sensitive to the fact that there may be some children who initially feel apprehensive. Gather the children together and play the music again

with the children sitting in a circle. Clap in time with the beat and ask the children to join in. Keep the beat and change to patting knees, thighs or the floor.
● Ask the children how the music makes them feel. Does it make them want to sit still or move about? Does it make them feel happy or sad? If it makes them feel happy, lively or excited, which colours do they associate with these feelings? Encourage them to listen to the music with you and to 'draw' the music in the air, making shapes, lines or dots.
● Show the children the large sheets of paper, sponges and paints. Tell them that you are going to play the music and you want them to use the

Learning objectives
Stepping Stones
● Begin to use representation as a means of communication. **(CD)**
● Try to capture experiences and responses with music, dance, paint and other materials or words. **(CD)**
Early Learning Goal
● Express and communicate their ideas, thoughts and feelings by using a widening range of materials, suitable tools, imaginative and role play, movement, designing and making, and a variety of songs and musical instruments. **(CD)**

sponges to paint the colours and shapes that they feel as they listen to it. They can move to the music as they paint, take breaks from painting to dance and return to complete their work.

● When the paintings are finished, ask the children to talk about the colours and shapes they have used and what they were trying to achieve. Display the paintings and leave the music player nearby so that the children can choose to listen to the music or dance as they look at and talk about their work.

Support and extension

● Show younger children how to dab the sponges into paint and wipe off the excess before painting.

● Tell older children to mix pots of colour by themselves after listening to the music, talking about the colours they want to use.

Further activities

● Choose a piece of calming music, as a complete contrast, such as Buddhist chants. Let the children lie down in a quiet space

and become immersed in the sounds. Later, ask them to choose colours and to paint what they feel as they listen to the music. Keep the atmosphere calm and peaceful throughout the activity.

● Provide a range of musical instruments and ask the children to select and play an instrument as they listen to one of the pieces of music.

Play link

Leave a music player and a diverse collection of music for the children to play and respond to in their own ways, plus paper, paints and crayons to encourage mark-making. **(CD)**

Home link

Suggest that parents and carers find a few minutes in the day to enjoy singing songs and nursery rhymes with their children, perhaps at bedtime or when walking to the setting.

Cross-curricular links
Stepping Stones
● Move freely with pleasure and confidence. **(PD)**
● Use movement to express feelings. **(PD)**
Early Learning Goal
● Move with confidence, imagination and in safety. **(PD)**

Artists

Children are introduced to the work of the artist, Mondrian. They talk about what they see and become artists themselves as they take inspiration from his work and produce their own paintings based on straight lines and blocks of colour.

Early painters identify straight lines in Mondrian's work and around the setting, and then use narrow rollers to paint their own straight lines.
More confident painters produce a large painting as a group, inspired by Mondrian's work.

What you need

Reproductions of work by Mondrian, including *Composition with Red, Yellow and Blue*; narrow rollers; black paint; red, yellow and blue rectangles of paper in assorted sizes; glue; 'I am an artist' badges; large piece of paper.

What to do

● Show the children reproductions of examples of work by Mondrian, including *Composition with Red, Yellow and Blue*. Do the pictures remind the children of anything? Talk about the meaning of the word 'artist' and tell the children that when they paint a picture they are artists too. Encourage the children to trace their fingers along the straight lines in the picture.

● Ask them to look for examples of straight lines around the setting, both inside and outside, and to trace their fingers along the lines to help them understand what 'straight' is like. Can they walk in a straight line or make straight lines with their arms, or line up in a straight line?

● Refer to the reproductions of the work of Mondrian and tell the children that you want them to be artists and make one very big picture together that is made of straight lines. Ask them which colours Mondrian used and say that you want them to use the same colours.

● Show the children the large piece of paper, narrow rollers and red, blue and yellow rectangles. Explain that you want them to use the rollers and black paint to create straight lines

Learning objectives
Stepping Stone
● Differentiate marks and movements on paper. **(CD)**
Early Learning Goal
● Explore colour, texture, shape, form and space in two or three dimensions. **(CD)**

and, when the paint is dry, to add the coloured rectangles and glue them in place. The aim is that the children take inspiration from the artist's work, not reproduce it.

● When they have finished, ask the children to compare their painting with Mondrian's work and talk about any similarities and differences they notice. Give the children their 'I am an artist' badges to wear for the rest of the session.

Support and extension
● Younger children can paint black lines with rollers on smaller pieces of paper with adult support.
● Older children can work together in a group using a large piece of paper, talking about what they want to do and making decisions together.

Further activities
● Give the children the opportunity to experiment in using different colours to create a painting in a similar style to the main activity. They could paint white lines on black paper and use silver and gold for the blocks of colour, or paint multicoloured lines

and add the blocks of colour in black.
● Make a large picture in the same style outdoors, using skipping ropes to make the lines and beanbags or fabric to make the blocks of colour. Let the children move the ropes and colours so that the artwork is constantly evolving.

Play link
Make an artists' corner by putting strips of black paper, rectangles of red, blue and yellow paper, small pieces of card and glue on a table for the children to use to make postcard-size pictures in a similar style to Mondrian's work. **(CD)**

Home link
Explain to parents and carers what their children have been doing and suggest that they help their children identify straight lines in their homes.

Cross-curricular links
Stepping Stones
● Demonstrate increasing skill and control in the use of mark-making implements, blocks, construction sets and 'small-world' activities. **(PD)**
● Show awareness of similarities in shapes in the environment. **(MD)**
Early Learning Goals
● Handle tools, objects, construction and malleable materials safely and with increasing control. **(PD)**
● Talk about, recognise and recreate simple patterns. **(MD)**

Pushing the boundaries

Chocolate paint

The children prepare cakes and chocolates for a special occasion by swirling different coloured cake mixtures together before cooking, and swirl melted chocolate 'paint' to create patterns.

Early painters use larger quantities as they swirl the cake mixture and chocolate using the handle end of spoons. **More confident painters** work on a smaller scale, making individual cakes with chocolate 'paint' on the top.

What you need
Ingredients and recipe to make a Victoria sponge cake; cocoa; red food colouring; spoons; plain, milk and white chocolate; aprons; hand-washing facilities; three mixing bowls; three small bowls; scales; shallow baking tin; oven; large flat plate or shallow dish; lollipop sticks.

What to do
● Plan a party with the children. Ask them to list the things they will need, such as: food, drinks, party hats and music. Suggest to the children that they make a special

cake and special chocolates to eat.
● Before handling any food, ensure that all surfaces are clean and that the children have washed their hands and are wearing aprons. Check beforehand if the children have any food allergies or dietary requirements.
● Start by making the cake. Read a recipe for a Victoria sponge cake with the children and let them help measure the ingredients and mix it. Ask the children to describe the mixture's colour and consistency as they stir it. Tell them that you would like them to make a cake that is a mixture of colours that are

Learning objectives
Stepping Stone
● Further explore an experience using a range of senses. **(CD)**
Early Learning Goal
● Respond in a variety of ways to what they see, hear, smell, touch and feel. **(CD)**

swirled together like paints being mixed. How could they do that? Listen to their ideas and, if it has not already been suggested, invite them to put some of the cake mixture into two other bowls. Flavour one with cocoa to make a chocolate mixture or brown 'paint', and add red colouring to the third bowl to make pink 'paint'.

● Ask the children to put spoonfuls of the yellow, pink and brown 'paints' into the same shallow baking tin. Using the handle end of a spoon, show the children how to swirl the mixtures together, taking care to still leave the separate colours visible. Bake as normal. When the cake is cool, cut it into pieces and serve it at the children's party.

● To 'paint' with chocolate, you will need to melt plain, milk and white chocolate in three separate bowls. Compare the chocolate before and after heating. Ensure it is not too hot before letting the children enjoy mixing the melted chocolate, describing its appearance, smell and texture. Put spoonfuls of each type of chocolate 'paint' quite close together on a plate or shallow dish. Encourage the children to create swirls and patterns as they mix the chocolate paints together using a lollipop stick. When set, break the chocolate into small pieces and serve at the party.

Support and extension

● Younger children may find it easier if they use twice as much cake mixture and chocolate, making big swirling patterns with the handle of a larger spoon.

● Older children can experiment in making individual multicoloured cakes in muffin tins and swirl chocolate 'paint' on the top when cold.

Further activities

● Make pools of ready-mixed paints in the three chocolate colours, on a large sheet of paper. Ask the children to use their fingers to create swirling patterns in the paint, as they did in the melted chocolate.

● Provide play dough in the three colours used in the cake. Ask the children to roll the dough into long 'sausages' and use these to create swirling patterns.

Play link

Provide paper, spoons and tubs of paint in a range of colours. Encourage the children to experiment by spooning blobs of paint close together onto the paper and making patterns by mixing the paints together, using objects such as sticks, pencils, forks or rulers. **(CD)**

Home link

Invite parents and carers to join the children at the party enjoying the cake and chocolate they made.

Cross-curricular links
Stepping Stone
● Display high levels of involvement in activities. **(PSED)**
Early Learning Goal
● Be confident to try new activities, initiate ideas and speak in a familiar group. **(PSED)**

Painting with sounds

The children learn to listen carefully, discriminate between sounds and then experiment in making sounds themselves with objects and voices, to paint a sound picture of a street scene.

Early painters make sounds as they play in a street-scene role-play area. These are recorded for them to listen to and identify later.
More confident painters experiment in making the sounds of a variety of footsteps walking and running.

What you need
Equipment to make the sounds of a street scene in the role-play area, such as: ride-on vehicles, large tray of gravel, portable radio, coconut shells, wooden blocks, washboard; tape recorder; selection of boots and shoes.

What to do
● Go for a walk in the local environment and stop in a safe place in a busy area, if possible. Ask the children to look around and tell you what they can see. Then ask them to close their eyes and tell you what they can hear. Depending on the position of the setting, the sounds they hear will obviously vary, but may include the sounds of vehicles, voices, footsteps, a dog barking, or baby crying.
● When you return to the setting, talk about the sounds you heard and set up a simple

street-scene role-play area to include ride-on vehicles with horns to beep, bicycles or tricycles with bells to ring, a radio, a large tray of gravel to use to make the sound of footsteps, coconut shells to make the sound of horses' hooves, and wooden blocks or a washboard to make the sound of things banging or clattering. As the children enjoy their role play, ask them about the sounds they are making and the sounds they can hear.
● Gather the children together and explain that you want them to paint a picture of the sounds they heard on their walk, but they will not be using any paint: they will be making a 'sound picture'.

Learning objectives
Stepping Stones
● Engage in imaginative and role play based on own first-hand experiences. **(CD)**
● Explore and learn how sounds can be changed. **(CD)**
Early Learning Goals
● Use their imagination in art and design, music, dance, imaginative and role play and stories. **(CD)**
● Recognise and explore how sounds can be changed, sing simple songs from memory, recognise repeated sounds and sound patterns and match movements to music. **(CD)**

● Use the items from the role-play area and improvise with other equipment from around the setting, to begin to make the sound picture together. Experiment with voices to make the sounds of cars braking, a baby crying, a dog barking, sirens on emergency vehicles or a train passing. Practise it a few times before finally recording the sound picture on the tape recorder. Then play it back, asking the children to identify the sounds they have made.

Support and extension
● Record younger children playing and enjoying making sounds in the role-play area. Play this back to the children and ask them to try and identify the sounds.
● Ask older children to experiment by adding the sounds of different types of footsteps on a pavement, such as stiletto heels, heavy boots or ordinary shoes. They can vary the speed of the footsteps from walking slowly to running.

Further activities
● Make a sound picture of a contrasting place such as inside a café. The children

can record the sounds of voices, a drink being poured into a cup, cutlery on plates, money being dropped into a till, doors banging and chairs scraping.
● Ask the children to collect items from around the setting to create their own sound picture. Participate in the role play, encouraging the children to listen to and comment on the sounds they are making.

Play link
Provide a collection of percussion instruments for the children to use as they experiment in making different sounds. Show them how to record the sounds they are making and play back the recording. **(CD)**

Home link
Suggest to parents and carers that bathtime is a good opportunity for their children to make and listen to different sounds as they splash, drip and pour water.

Cross-curricular links
Stepping Stone
● Respond to simple instructions. **(CLL)**
Early Learning Goal
● Sustain attentive listening, responding to what they have heard by relevant comments, questions and actions. **(CLL)**

Painting with fabric

The children use voile as a giant's paint palette, placing one colour on top of another and painting lines and shapes.

Early painters experience the beauty of the colours and make shapes and lines with support.
More confident painters draw large shapes with chalk on the floor and fill the shapes with the fabric colour.

What you need
Approximately six 3m lengths of voile in a range of vibrant colours; digital camera; rubber bands.

What to do
● Hold the ends of the fabric lengths together and secure with a rubber band. Suspend the bundle of fabrics so that approximately half of the fabric lies on the floor. Drape these attractively together.
● Show the children the fabrics. Let them handle, drape, twist and overlap them. Talk about the texture, colours and the fact that the children can see through them. Remove the rubber band and let the children experiment freely with the material. They can wrap themselves in fabric, swirl it in the air, look through it or scrunch it up and feel it against their faces.

● When they have had time to enjoy the properties of the fabric, ask the children to lay the pieces next to each other in a straight line. Suggest that the colours look like lines that have been painted with a giant brush. Tell the children that you want them to think of the fabrics as paints in a giant's paintbox. Ask them to imagine that they are the giant and think of different lines and shapes he might want to paint. Give them the opportunity to create designs, placing the colours they choose next to each other on the floor.
● When the children have had time to experiment, tell them that you want them to make one giant painting together, using all of the fabrics and thinking about the colours they put next to each other. They could lay

Learning objectives
Stepping Stone
● Make constructions, collages, paintings, drawings and dances. (CD)
Early Learning Goal
● Explore colour, texture, shape, form and space in two or three dimensions. (CD)

the fabrics flat and overlap them, bunch them up and place them close together like textured paint or use them to paint shapes, lines and spirals. Watch how the children work, listen to their comments and only intervene if they need help.

● When completed, ask the children to describe what they were trying to do and whether they feel they achieved their aim. Encourage them to talk about the colours. Photograph their work as a record and talking point to be used later.

Support and extension

● Younger children may need shorter lengths of voile and support in arranging the fabric.

● Older children can draw large shapes onto a floor or play area with chalk and use the fabric to paint over the lines or fill spaces.

Further activities

● Give each child a small piece of voile or a scarf made from a delicate fabric. Play a variety of dance music and let the children interpret the music, moving freely as they incorporate the piece of fabric into their dance.

● Turn a small table upside down and weave the fabrics around the table legs to make a 3D painting. Ask the children to think about the colours they want to put next to each other and talk about the result. Remind them to take care as they work around the legs of the table.

Play link

Leave the fabrics in a basket with a box of rings that are used with curtain poles. The children can experiment in using the fabrics for dressing up and role play, using the rings as fasteners, as they pull the fabric through them. Alternatively they can mix the colours and make shapes by pulling different fabrics through the rings. **(CD)**

Home link

Invite parents and carers to look at the photographs of the work and discuss what the children have done.

Cross-curricular links
Stepping Stone
● Construct with large materials such as cartons, long lengths of fabric and planks. **(PD)**
Early Learning Goal
● Use a range of small and large equipment. **(PD)**

Painting with words

No paint is used in this activity, as the children are asked to paint with words. They eat ice creams, describing them using their senses, in order to paint a colourful word picture.

What you need

Rug; ice-cream cornets; toppings; digital camera; photocopiable page 55 'Ice-cream ideas'; pencils.

What to do

● Check first with parents and carers if the children have any food allergies or dietary requirements. Spread a rug outside on a warm day.

Explain that you have ice creams for the children to eat and you want them to paint a picture with words, describing the ice cream's appearance, taste, texture and smell.

● Provide each child with an identical ice cream in a cornet. If possible, use more than one flavour of ice cream and add a topping to give more scope in the description. Take a photograph of one of the ice creams.

● Ask the children to give you words or phrases to describe the ice creams. Write these words onto the outline of the ice-cream cornet on the photocopiable sheet.

● Later, read the description to another group of children and ask if the words paint

> **Early painters** enjoy the ice creams and contribute words with support.
> **More confident painters** paint a word picture, writing their words onto an outline of an ice cream.

a picture in their heads. Let them draw a picture of the ice cream. Show the children the photograph – is it what they imagined?

Support and extension

● Younger children may need support in suggesting words and a shorter time spent on the descriptions.
● Older children can help to write their descriptive words on the ice-cream outline and read these to another group of children.

Further activities

● Fill five containers with a variety of contrasting materials, such as: grit, fir cones, aluminium foil, fake fur fabric and marbles. Ask the children to paint a picture in words for each.
● Take the children outside on a frosty, snowy, rainy or windy day. Later, ask them to paint a picture in words of the weather.

Home link

Parents and carers can extend their children's vocabulary by encouraging them to describe something they pass when walking to the setting.

> **Learning objectives**
> **Stepping Stones**
> ● Try to capture experiences and responses with music, dance, paint and other materials or words. **(CD)**
> ● Show an interest in what they see, hear, smell, touch and feel. **(CD)**
> **Early Learning Goal**
> ● Respond in a variety of ways to what they see, hear, smell, touch and feel. **(CD)**

> **Cross-curricular links**
> **Stepping Stone**
> ● Build up vocabulary that reflects the breadth of their experiences. **(CLL)**
> **Early Learning Goal**
> ● Extend their vocabulary, exploring the meanings and sounds of new words. **(CLL)**

Ice-cream ideas

At the beach

In this summer-time activity, the children enjoy playing in the sand in a beach role-play area, before painting a large beach picture together using a variety of resources representing painted areas. They are encouraged to think about their choices in colour and texture.

Early painters experience colour and texture as they select materials.
More confident painters search for and choose additional resources to add to their picture.

What you need
Stories and poems about the seaside; sand tray; buckets; spades; picnic basket; shells; pretend seaweed; water tray; small-world seaside animals, including crabs and fish; basket; coloured Cellophane; assorted papers and card; chalk; digital camera.

What to do
● Read stories and poems to the children about the seaside and talk about their experiences of seaside holidays. Set up a beach role-play area inside or outside the setting. If practical, this should include sand in which the children can actually sit, stand or play. Try to include items, such as: a water tray, buckets and spades, a picnic

basket, shells, sand, pretend seaweed, and small-world animals, such as crabs and fish.
● Participate in the play, encouraging the children to feel the textures and talk about the colours of the sand, shells and seaweed. Provide a basket of resources with coloured Cellophane, assorted papers and card in 'beach' colours. Use chalk to draw a large 'picture frame' on a path or play area and tell the children that you want them to paint a big seaside picture together, but instead of using their usual paints they will be using the materials in the basket as blocks of colour to make the picture. As the items will not be glued in place, tell the children that

Learning objectives
Stepping Stones
● Choose particular colours to use for a purpose. **(CD)**
● Experiment to create different textures. **(CD)**
Early Learning Goal
● Explore colour, texture, shape, form and space in two or three dimensions. **(CD)**

you will photograph the picture before dismantling it.

● Encourage the children to think about the colours they associate with the beach and select these colours to make their picture. They can include pieces of paper and Cellophane to represent the sea, sky, Sun and sand. The children may choose to use the resources to create patterns, an abstract collage or a picture of a beach scene. Ask them to talk about the colours and textures they have used, giving reasons for their choices. Encourage the children to reflect on what they have done and discuss any changes they want to make.

Support and extension
● Younger children may prefer to make their own pictures on a small mat or tray.
● Ask older children to look for other materials to use in their pictures from around the setting, taking into consideration texture and colour.

Further activities
● Provide a selection of resources that the children can use to create a collage picture of the sea. These could include: clear plastic, tissue paper, voile, ribbons, lace,

sequins and shiny threads. The children can arrange these and glue them onto paper.
● Ask the children which colours they associate with the sea and sand. Give them time to experiment in mixing these colours with powder paint. Ask each child to cover a small square of paper with dots of paint applied with their fingers in their chosen seaside colours. When dry, mount all of the squares together to make one large picture.

Play link
Provide wet sand, buckets, spades, shells, stones and water. Show the children how to make a sandcastle with a 'moat' around it and ask them to experiment in making sandcastles, moats and rock pools. Ask questions such as: *When you fill a hole in sand with water, does it stay there? Where does it go?* **(KUW)**

Home link
Invite parents and carers to encourage imaginative play at home by setting up a simple picnic area in the home or garden for their children.

Cross-curricular links
Stepping Stone
● Talk activities through, reflecting on and modifying what they are doing. **(CLL)**
Early Learning Goal
● Use talk to organise, sequence and clarify thinking, ideas, feelings and events. **(CLL)**

Painting with photos

Children look closely at the colours and textures of the skin of fruits. They take close-up digital photographs of the fruit, print these and use them as 'paint' to make a picture.

Early painters examine a fruit using their senses and take photographs with adult support.
More confident painters have more responsibility for taking the photographs and experiment in using them as 'paint'.

What you need

Basket of fruits that have interesting textured skins, such as: pineapple, dragon fruit, pomegranate, lychee, star fruit and coconut; magnifiers; digital camera; computer; paper (photographic quality if possible); scissors; glue; plain paper or fabric; backing paper.

What to do

● Check for any food allergies before showing the children the basket of fruits and encourage them to touch, smell and talk about the colour and texture of each item. Ask them to use the magnifiers to look closely at the texture and patterns on the skins.
● Explain to the children that you want them to make a picture of one of the fruits, but instead of using paints they will be taking a lot of photographs of the fruit and using those as 'paint' to make the picture. Place the fruit they have chosen onto a piece of plain paper or fabric and help the children use a digital camera to take close-up photographs from different angles. Show them how to alter the camera settings so that they can look at the photographs they have just taken.
● Ask the children to help as you download the photographs onto the computer. Show them a slideshow of the photographs and let them help as you choose the sizes to print – 'business-card' size will give plenty of scope when they 'paint' with them later. Invite the children to select which photographs to print, and press the appropriate buttons. If possible, print

Learning objectives
Stepping Stones
● Begin to describe the texture of things. **(CD)**
● Make constructions, collages, paintings, drawings and dances. **(CD)**
Early Learning Goal
● Explore colour, texture, shape, form and space in two or three dimensions. **(CD)**

onto photographic paper for best results.
● Ask the children to trim around the edges of the photographs. It does not matter if the photographs are cut out unevenly. Let the children experiment in using the photographs as blocks of paint as they 'paint' a large fruit onto backing paper, sticking the pieces in place.

Support and extension
● Younger children may need one-to-one support in taking the photographs.
● Older children can experiment in 'painting' the name of the fruit using the close-up photographs.

Further activities
● Ask the children to take close-up photographs of the other fruits in the basket and show the photographs on the computer as a slideshow. Gather the children round and see if they can identify the fruits from the photographs.
● Arrange a fruit tasting session. Check with parents and carers first for any food allergies or dietary requirements and remind the children about washing their hands before handling food. Show them that you are using a clean board and knife to prepare the fruits. Encourage the children to try a little of each of the fruits used in the main activity, talking about their likes and dislikes. Discuss the fact that fruit makes a healthy and enjoyable snack.

Play link
Place a copy of *Handa's Surprise* by Eileen Browne (Walker Books) and one of each of the fruits mentioned in the story into a basket with paper, pencils, crayons and scissors. Encourage the children to share the story and draw the characters, fruits or animals mentioned in it. They can leave their drawings in the basket as a resource for others to look at and share. **(CLL)**

Home link
Suggest to parents and carers that they help their children identify fruits when out shopping and let them choose one piece of fruit as a treat.

Cross-curricular links
Stepping Stones
● Show an interest in ICT. **(KUW)**
● Know how to operate simple equipment. **(KUW)**
● Complete a simple program on the computer and/or perform simple functions on ICT apparatus. **(KUW)**
Early Learning Goal
● Find out about and identify the uses of everyday technology and use information and communication technology and programmable toys to support their learning. **(KUW)**

Painting on-screen

Children hold hands in a line and 'draw' shapes and enclose spaces, before transferring this idea to drawing and painting using a simple paint program on the computer.

Early painters learn how to draw simple shapes and fill them with colour, using the computer.
More confident painters choose and change 'line' and 'fill' colours as they paint their pictures on the computer.

What you need

Computer; simple paint program designed for young children; digital camera; printer; paper; coloured pencils; felt-tipped pens; crayons.

What to do

● Ask the children to join hands and look at the line they have formed. Is it straight or curved? Can they use that line to create a shape? Join the ends of the line together and make different shapes. Ask another adult to take photographs of the shapes you make. (Obtain parents' or carers' permission before taking photographs.) Encourage the children to think about the lines and shapes they have made by asking questions, such as: *What is in the middle of the shape? If it is an empty space, could we put something inside it?* The children can choose objects or other children to place

inside their shapes. Take more photographs as a record.

● Show the children the photographs of the shapes they have made. Tell them that you want them to think of each of the photographs as a picture. Which picture do they like best and why? Explain that in these pictures they drew the lines using their bodies instead of a pencil. How else could they draw shapes with something inside them? Have a range of drawing media for the children to use, and encourage and praise lateral thinking. For example, children can draw on a steamy window, in sand in the sand tray, or arrange dolls, bricks or cars into shapes.

● When you have discussed their ideas, tell the children that there is

Learning objectives
Stepping Stones
● Use lines to enclose a space, then begin to use these shapes to represent objects. **(CD)**
● Choose particular colours to use for a purpose. **(CD)**
Early Learning Goal
● Explore colour, texture, shape, form and space in two or three dimensions. **(CD)**

another way they could draw shapes. Suggest that they use a paint program on the computer. Depending on their experience in using a computer, you may need to show the children how to move the mouse to make the pointer move on the screen and to click the left button to choose a colour and drawing tool. When drawing, they will need to hold down the left button to create a line. Give the children time to experiment in choosing colours, painting shapes and then painting dots or other shapes inside them. Help them to print their work.

● Talk to the children about which medium they enjoyed using most, giving their reasons.

Support and extension

● Younger children may need one-to-one support in using the paint program.
● Encourage older children to choose and change the colours when using the 'line' and 'fill' tools.

Further activities

● As the children become confident with the computer, show them how to use the 'shape' tools and fill the shapes with colour.
● Ask the children to use a paint program to create a picture as part of a cross-curricular theme. For example, as part of a weather theme, they could paint the Sun, choosing the appropriate colours and fitting the Sun shape into the space available on-screen.

Play link

Laminate cards with simple coloured shapes drawn on them using a paint program. Ask the children to choose a shape and try and create the same shapes on-screen. When they have drawn the shape, they can add lines and colours to change it into something else, such as a face or animal. **(KUW)**

Home link

Involve parents and carers by inviting them to spend time watching their children use a paint program.

Cross-curricular links
Stepping Stones
● Show an interest in ICT. **(KUW)**
● Complete a simple program on the computer and/or perform simple functions on ICT apparatus. **(KUW)**
Early Learning Goal
● Find out about and identify the uses of everyday technology and use information and communication technology and programmable toys to support their learning. **(KUW)**

A living painting

In this activity the children 'paint' a picture of what happens in a nursery rhyme, by setting the scene and taking the roles of the characters in a simple tableau. They make props and dress up as the characters. The 'painting' is photographed as a record.

Early painters participate in the tableau or living painting using ready-prepared props.
More confident painters help choose and make props as they set the scene for the living painting.

What you need

Favourite nursery rhyme; digital camera; materials to make a range of props, such as: boxes, plastic containers, labels, coloured card, fabric, paint, paintbrushes, rollers, glue and so on; paper; pencils.

What to do

● Choose a traditional nursery rhyme that the children enjoy, such as 'Sing a Song of Sixpence'. Go through the rhyme and draw simple pictures of the main events in it:
  ● the blackbirds in the pie
  ● the king counting the money
  ● the queen eating bread and honey
  ● the maid hanging out the clothes
  ● the blackbird pecking her nose.
● Ask the children to name and describe the characters and retell what happens. Say that you want them to pretend to be the different characters. Repeat the rhyme together with the children role playing the different parts. Ask the children to tell you which props they need to help them bring the rhyme to life. For example, these could include a pie, table and chairs for the king and queen, money, bread and honey, washing on a line, and clothes for dressing up as the characters.
● Encourage the children to help make the props.

Learning objectives
Stepping Stones
● Use available resources to create props to support role play. **(CD)**
● Play cooperatively as part of a group to act out a narrative. **(CD)**
Early Learning Goal
● Use their imagination in art and design, music, dance, imaginative and role play and stories. **(CD)**

These can be as simple or elaborate as you choose. For example, the children can use rollers to paint the sides of the pie, make a label for a pot of honey and use sponge cleaning-pads for 'bread'. The blackbird's 'beak' can be made from small cones painted yellow with elastic to hold them in place. They can make crowns for the king and queen, and use lengths of fabric for cloaks.

● Tell the children that you want them to 'paint' a big picture by using the items they have made and getting into the picture themselves as the characters in the rhyme. When everything and everyone is in place, tell the children that it looks just like an illustration in a book of nursery rhymes. Take a photograph and display it next to a copy of the rhyme. (Obtain parents' or carers' pemission before taking photographs.) Encourage the children to talk about the finished result.

Support and extension
● Younger children can use simple ready-prepared props when creating their picture.
● Invite older children to arrange several 'sets', moving the props and characters to make different pictures to photograph.

Further activities
● Make living paintings that fit in with a cross-curricular theme, for example, 'The seaside'. The children can decide what they need in the picture, such as: sand, shells, buckets and spades.
● Make a book of living paintings over the course of a few months with titles written by the children. The book could be on a theme, for example, 'Rhymes and poems', or linked to a particular season.

Play link
Provide a box of assorted dolls, paper, pens, scissors and other props that the children can use to make up their own 'paintings' linked to work being covered in other areas. **(CD)**

Home link
Leave the book of living paintings available for parents and carers to share when they collect their children.

Cross-curricular links
Stepping Stones
● Listen to favourite nursery rhymes, stories and songs. Join in with repeated refrains, anticipating key events and important phrases. **(CLL)**
● Describe main story settings, events and principal characters. **(CLL)**
Early Learning Goal
● Listen with enjoyment, and respond to stories, songs and other music, rhymes and poems and make up their own stories, songs, rhymes and poems. **(CLL)**

■SCHOLASTIC

In this series:

ISBN 978-0439-94499-1   ISBN 978-0439-945158

To find out more, call: 0845 603 9091
or visit our website www.scholastic.co.uk